The Baby Boomer

OR

How to Eat Cheaper Than Dog Food

Photos by Joy Jameson

A Guide to Inexpensive Culinary Delights

BOOKSURGE, LLC
AN AMAZON.COM COMPANY

© 2005 by Joy Jameson. All Rights Reserved.

Published and distributed by:

BookSurge, LLC
An Amazon.com Company
1.866.308.6235
www.booksurgepublishing.com

ISBN 1-4196-1480-0

Dedication

This book is dedicated to my siblings, Dee, Sue, Mick, Linda & Lisa, who are always there for me, whether I need them or not.

Table of Contents

Introduction   vii

Money Saving Tips   ix

Dog Food Cost Table   x

Main Courses
- Breakfast Pizza   3
- Chicken Alfredo   4
- Chicken Bruschetta Sandwiches   5
- Frittata with Mushrooms and Basil   6
- Garlic Chicken Thighs with Potatoes   8
- Ham and Spinach Pasta   9
- Ham and Swiss Pie   10
- Lemon Pasta with Shrimp   12
- Three Cheese Lasagna   14
- Steamed Fish with Orange Sauce   16
- Sausage and Onion Calzones   18
- Grilled Polenta with Garlic Tomato Sauce   20
- Meatball Sandwiches   22
- Pork Burritos   24
- Puttanesca with Bacon, Tomatoes and Basil   25
- Lemon Pepper Turkey Pitas   26

Soups
- Bean Soup with Ham   29
- Grandma's Chicken Soup   30
- Chunky Tomato Soup   32
- Potato Soup with Swiss Cheese and Ham   33
- Savory Mushroom Soup   34

Salads
- BBQ Chicken Salad   37
- Fig Salad   38
- Greens with Cranberries and Walnuts   39
- Pomegranate and Pear Salad   40

Sweet Treats
- Baked Pears in Wine   43
- Cinnamon Berry Crepes   44
- Hazelnut Meringues   46
- Trail Mix Cookies   48
- Coffee Granita   50

Jake's Favorite Dog Biscuits   51

Price Calculation Rules   52

Ingredient Prices   54

Introduction

The conversation at our dinner table for the last few years always turned to the topic of how we would be able to afford to eat when or if we were ever able to retire. Inevitably we would comment that we would just have to eat dog food. Though I had tasted dog food in my youth, the thought of a steady diet did not sound that appealing to me. For those of you who buy dog food regularly, I am sure you would agree that the cost of dog food is not exactly cheap, especially the gourmet kind that is suppose to be so good for your dog's health and well being. Through the years of living rather frugally, we developed quite a few menus that would make us exclaim with some pride that the meal we were enjoying **had to be cheaper than dog food!** Maybe, just maybe we could retire someday knowing we could afford a good meal on a regular basis without breaking the bank.

I have the great fortune of living in southern California. While it is true that most things are higher in price, food is not. Fresh ingredients can be had year round for a reasonable cost. However, I find that shopping and comparing prices is still critical to ensure savings. I do most of my shopping in the following stores: Vons, Costco, Henry's, Plowboy's, Trader Joes and Big Lots. Vons is a big grocery store chain here in California. While it has a bit of everything, I always use coupons when shopping there because they double them. This can be a great savings and is worth every bit of time it takes to clip them out of the paper. I also always check their sales before buying, especially when buying meat. On average I save between 30 and 40% each time I shop there by using coupons and shopping sales. Henry's, Plowboy's and Trader Joes are small chains but have great produce, cheap grains, and dairy. Costco is another great source if you are able to use vast quantities before it spoils. Eggs, butter, meat, dry goods and canned goods are a great buy. Don't overlook Big Lots for some real savings. Although their selection is limited, and certain items may not be available the next time you shop, you will find bargains galore.

I began this book as a way to document the cost of some of our favorite meals. I found the task to be a pleasure because, to put it simply, I love food! I love thinking about it, reading about it, shopping for it, preparing it and planning for each meal. I love feeling victorious when I think I have snagged a real bargain. I also loved comparing prices and writing this book. After trying some of the recipes and inventing your own, I hope you will agree that everyone, with a little ingenuity, **can indeed eat cheaper than dog food!**

Money Saving Tips

1. **Buy a freezer.** A freezer is the most important money saving investment you can make.

2. **Buy in bulk.** Items bought in bulk are far cheaper per ounce than those bought in smaller quantities. The following items should be frozen for longer storage.
   - **Flour** - I buy 25 lbs at a time. Keep it in containers with tight lids to keep flour bugs from finding it. It is important to freeze wheat flour because it can go rancid.
   - **Sugar** - Brown, granulated, and powdered sugar have a long shelf life. Keep brown sugar tightly closed so it doesn't dry out and become hard.
   - **Butter** - Buy butter in 1 pound blocks. I buy boxes that contain 4 one pound blocks. When using it, I weigh my amounts. One cup of butter equals 8 ounces.
   - **Nuts** - Nuts stay fresher longer when frozen as they can also go rancid. The flavor is intensified when roasted, so roast some ahead of time and keep frozen until needed.
   - **Can tomatoes, tomato sauce, and tomato paste** - Buy the largest size available, then divide it and freeze it in baggies. This technique is especially money saving for tomato paste. Many recipes call for just a tablespoon or two, and then I am stuck with the rest of the can. I freeze tomato paste in ¼ cup portions.
   - **Yeast** - The small packets are incredibly expensive per ounce. If you do a lot of baking, buy it by the jar or pound and keep it in your refrigerator or freezer. Even if you do not use it all by the expiration date you will probably still save money with the larger quantity.

3. **Buy eggs in cartons of 18.** Freeze extra egg yolks as well as egg whites. They are fine for omelets as well as for most baking purposes. Eggs yolks are great to use in dog biscuit recipes.

4. **Don't throw away fruit that is too ripe.** Wrap and freeze it. Frozen fruit is great for smoothies or pies.

5. **Always read the grocery store sale ads.** Use coupons. I collect coupons and then use them on a sale item in a store that doubles my coupon. This strategy is great for personal hygeine items such as toothpaste. I pay as little as 29¢ for brand name toothpaste. You will have more money left over for food items.

6. **Stock up on items that are on sale.** When whole chickens are 55¢ a pound, buy several.

7. Keep chicken and turkey carcasses, as well as ham bones in the freezer until you have time to boil them for broth and soups. There is nothing better than bean soup made with a ham bone.

8. Learn to like chicken thighs. Thighs are more cost effective than breasts and dark meat is tastier besides.

9. Don't be tempted to buy grated cheese. Grate your own and enjoy the savings. Consider freezing cheese if you have a large quantity to prevent waste from mold. Freezing may change the texture but it is fine to use.

10. Grow your own spices. It is easy to grow basil, rosemary, chives, mint and parsley. There is no substitute for fresh spices. If you have to buy them, wrap them in a damp paper towel and then wrap them in plastic. Keep them in the refrigerator.

11. Don't throw away the end slices of bread. Freeze these along with other pieces of bread you may not consider sandwich worthy. After you have accumulated a sack full, put them in a food processor and make your own bread crumbs.

12. If you own a dog, consider making dog biscuits instead of buying them. There are hundreds of dog biscuit recipes. It is a great way to use up any extra egg yolks you may have accumulated.

Dog Food Cost

My dog Jake is a 70 pound, 9 year old, hungry Dalmatian. According to the directions on the cans, he should receive anywhere from 2 cans of food to 28 trays of gourmet food a day, depending of course on the brand of the food. Since most major brands specify the amount a dog should eat based on weight, I have based the cost of his meal accordingly. The following is a sampling of the various varieties available.*

Brand	Price per oz	Serving Size for Jake	Cost per serving
ALPO Prime Cuts	$0.05	2 ½ cans (22 oz each)	$2.75
Atta Boy Vita Snacks	$0.66	1 stick (.3 oz)	$0.20
Beggin Strips	$0.63	1 strip (.4 oz)	$0.25
IAMS	$0.09	2 cans (14 oz each)	$2.52
IAMS dog biscuits	$0.14	2 biscuits (1.1 oz each)	$0.31
Kibbles & Bits	$0.06	2 cans (22 oz each)	$2.64
Lots O Tbonz	$0.26	1 treat (.4 oz)	$0.10
Pedigree	$0.06	2 ¼ cans (22 oz each)	$2.97
Pedigree Cesar Select**	$0.27	28 trays (4 trays per 10 lbs, 3.5 oz each)	$26.46
Purina Mighty Dog**	$0.16	14 cans (1 can per 5 lbs, 5.5 oz each)	$12.32
Soft & Smart	$0.05	5 pouches (6 oz each)	$1.50

* The prices quoted above were gathered in the month of November 2004 and are subject to change. Dog food, like anything else, goes on sale from time to time.

** These are recommended for small dogs, perhaps because the cost is prohibitive for large dogs.

x

Main Courses

Breakfast Pizza
2 servings @ 55¢ per serving

I had a similar dish in a restaurant and found it to be a much more interesting item then the usual omelet. Not only is it very good, it is very appealing to look at! You could vary the items you add to suit your taste.

Ingredient	Cost	Cost per recipe
2 eggs	$0.06 each	$0.12
1 tomato (3 oz), sliced	$0.06 per ounce	$0.18
⅛ cup (5 leaves) fresh basil, chiffonade	$0.50 per ounce	$0.05
¼ cup (1 oz) Romano cheese, grated	$0.29 per ounce	$0.29
Total Cost		**$1.09**

1. Beat eggs in a small bowl.

2. Heat a 7" skillet on medium high. Coat pan with cooking spray.

3. Pour eggs in the pan and cook until set.

4. Add the tomato slices, basil and cheese. Cover the pan for a minute until the cheese begins to melt. Add salt if desired.

Chicken Alfredo
4 servings @ $1.61 per serving

This is my favorite company dish. I haven't served it to anyone yet who wasn't wild about it. I like to grill the chicken, but baked would do just as well. Be sure to use fresh grated Parmesan cheese and not the "stuff" in a can as the texture will be gritty.

Ingredient	Cost	Cost per recipe
2 (8 oz each) chicken breasts, boneless	$0.12 per ounce	$1.92
1 tablespoon (.5 oz) olive oil	$0.13 per ounce	$0.07
1 teaspoon (<.1 oz) cayenne pepper	$0.43 per ounce	$0.01
½ cup (4 oz) cream	$0.09 per ounce	$0.36
½ cup (4 oz) butter	$0.12 per ounce	$0.48
1 cup (4 oz) Parmesan cheese, grated	$0.66 per ounce	$2.64
Salt and pepper to taste	$0.00	$0.00
1 tablespoon (<.1 oz) parsley, chopped	$0.06 per ounce	$0.01
1 pound fettuccine	$0.06 per ounce	$0.96
Total Cost		**$6.45**

1. Brush a little olive oil on each breast and sprinkle with cayenne pepper. Grill, about 10 minutes per side or until cooked through. Slice into strips and set aside.

2. Combine cream and butter in a saucepan and heat until butter is melted.

3. Add cheese to cream mixture, a little at a time, stirring constantly until melted.

3. Add salt, pepper and parsley.

5. Cook fettuccine according to package directions and drain.

6. Pour sauce over pasta and toss.

7. Put the dog outside while you eat so he doesn't slobber all over the floor.

Chicken Bruschetta Sandwiches
2 servings @ $1.95 per serving

This is no ho-hum sandwich. I like to use freshly made pesto whenever possible. However, when fresh basil is not to be found, the store bought will do.

Ingredient	Cost	Cost per recipe
1 tomato (3 oz), chopped	$0.06 per ounce	$0.18
¼ cup (1 oz) feta, crumbled	$0.17 per ounce	$0.17
2 green onions, sliced	$0.08 each	$0.16
1 tablespoon (.4 oz) balsamic vinegar	$0.11 per ounce	$0.04
1 tablespoon (.5 oz) olive oil	$0.09 per ounce	$0.05
2 (8 oz each) chicken breasts, boneless	$0.12 per ounce	$1.92
¼ cup (1 oz) pesto	$0.38 per ounce	$0.38
2 (4.5 oz each) sandwich rolls	$0.11 per ounce	$0.99
Total Cost		**$3.89**

1. Preheat grill.

2. Toss tomato, cheese and green onion with balsamic vinegar and olive oil.

3. Grill chicken, brushing lightly with a little pesto just before done.

4. Grill rolls until lightly browned.

5. Spread rolls with remaining pesto. Add chicken breast and top with tomato mixture.

Frittata with Mushrooms and Basil
4 servings @ 41¢ per serving

A frittata is a cross between a crustless quiche and an unfolded omelet. You can add any ingredients you would normally add to either a quiche or an omelet, or you can be creative and thrifty and empty your refrigerator of leftovers. I use leftover pasta that has not had sauce added whenever possible - a cost saving ingredient right there!

Ingredient	Cost	Cost per recipe
2 cups (5 oz) mushrooms, sliced	$0.12 per ounce	$0.60
2 green onions, sliced	$0.08 per onion	$0.16
½ cup (4 oz) milk	$0.02 per ounce	$0.08
1 tablespoon (.5 oz) butter, melted	$0.12 per ounce	$0.06
½ teaspoon salt	< $0.01 per ounce	$0.01
4 large eggs	$0.06 per egg	$0.24
2 cups cooked pasta (4.6 oz uncooked)	$0.03 per ounce	$0.14
¼ cup (10 leaves) fresh basil, chopped	$0.50 per ounce	$0.10
½ cup (2 oz) mozzarella cheese, grated	$0.13 per ounce	$0.26
Salt and pepper to taste	$0.00	$0.00
Total Cost		**$1.65**

1. Preheat oven to 450°.

2. Heat skillet over medium heat. Coat pan with cooking spray. Add mushrooms and onions. Sauté about 6 minutes or until tender, stirring frequently. Cool slightly.

3. Whisk the milk, butter, salt, and eggs together in a bowl. Add the onion mixture, cooked pasta and basil. Toss to combine.

4. Heat a 10" oven-proof skillet over medium-low heat. Coat skillet with cooking spray. Add the egg mixture and cook until edges begin to set. Gently lift the edge of the egg mixture to allow some uncooked mixture to come in contact with the pan. Cook until set, about 5 more minutes.

5. Sprinkle with cheese. Bake about 7 minutes or until golden brown. Cut into 4 wedges. Salt and pepper to taste.

Note: Other ingredients that work well in this recipe are leaks, yellow onion, sausage, bacon, spinach, artichokes, asparagus, broccoli, peppers, Romano, Parmesan or Swiss cheese.

Garlic Chicken Thighs with Potatoes
3 servings @ 91¢ per serving

If you don't like garlic, you probably won't like this dish. I like to use the roasted garlic in this dish as a spread for my bread. Don't have an important date planned for the end of the meal unless your date happens to be a garlic lover also.

Ingredient	Cost	Cost per recipe
6 chicken thighs (6 oz each)	$0.05 per ounce	$1.80
Salt and pepper to taste	$0.00	$0.00
½ cup (4 oz) olive oil	$0.13 per ounce	$0.52
2 heads of garlic (1.5 oz each)	$0.08 per ounce	$0.24
3 potatoes (1 lb), cubed	$0.01 per ounce	$0.16
Total Cost		**$2.72**

1. Preheat oven to 350° F.

2. Season chicken with salt and pepper.

3. Heat about 2 tablespoons of the olive oil in a large skillet over high heat. Add the chicken and brown well on both sides. It may be wise to use a splatter guard while frying.

4. Add the rest of the oil, the garlic and the potatoes. Cover and bake for 1 1/2 hours.

Note: Sprigs of rosemary or thyme can be added while baking for additional flavor.

Ham and Spinach Pasta
4 servings @ 72¢ per serving

This dish is one of my favorites and an excellent way to use left over ham. Be sure to drain as much water as possible from the spinach. I normally squeeze it by hand over the sink and then place it on a paper towel to help absorb the moisture.

Ingredient	Cost	Cost per recipe
1 pound frozen spinach	$0.07 per ounce	$1.12
¼ cup (2 oz) butter	$0.12 per ounce	$0.24
3 ounces ham, cooked and sliced	$0.06 per ounce	$0.18
6 tablespoons (3 oz) cream	$0.09 per ounce	$0.27
Freshly grated nutmeg to taste (< .1 oz)	$0.04 per ounce	$0.01
Salt and pepper to taste	$0.00	$0.00
1 pound pasta	$0.03 per ounce	$0.48
½ cup (2 oz) Romano cheese, grated	$0.29 per ounce	$0.58
Total Cost		**$2.88**

1. Thaw spinach. Squeeze the water out of the spinach with your hands, getting out as much liquid as possible.

2. Melt butter in a saucepan over medium heat.

3. Add the ham, cream and nutmeg and stir constantly a couple of minutes. Season with salt and pepper if desired.

4. Cook pasta according to directions and drain.

5. Toss pasta with ham and spinach mixture. Add the grated cheese and stir.

Ham and Swiss Pie
6 servings @ 56¢ per serving

This pie is the next thing to a sandwich and a lot less messy to eat. It is convenient to pack for picnics or lunches. It is just as good hot or cold.

Ingredient	Cost	Cost per recipe
2 cups (8 oz) all purpose flour	$0.01 per ounce	$0.08
½ cup (4 oz) butter, cubed	$0.12 per ounce	$0.48
Pinch of salt	$0.00	$0.00
4 eggs	$0.06 per egg	$0.24
⅛ cup water	$0.00	$0.00
¼ cup (2.5 oz) ounces mustard	$0.03 per ounce	$0.08
8 ounces cooked ham, chopped	$0.06 per ounce	$0.48
2 cups (8 oz) Swiss cheese, grated	$0.25 per ounce	$2.00
Total Cost		**$3.36**

1. Preheat oven to 425° F.

2. Combine the flour, butter and salt in a mixing bowl using the paddle attachment. Add 2 of the eggs and water and mix to form a smooth soft ball.

3. Divide the dough into two equal pieces. Roll one piece into a circle until it is big enough to line an 11" tart pan.

4. Spread the mustard evenly on the bottom of the dough.

5. Layer the ham and cheese on top of the mustard.

6. Beat the remaining two eggs and pour them on the ham and cheese, reserving a small amount to brush on the top dough.

7. Roll the remaining piece of dough until it is large enough to fit on top of the tart.

8. Using a rolling pin, lightly roll over the top of the tart, cutting away the excess crust.

9. Brush the top with the reserved egg. Bake until golden brown, about 40 minutes. Allow it to rest before cutting.

Lemon Pasta with Shrimp
4 servings @ $2.08 per serving

When I first became aware that lemons and cream could be combined to make a tasty dish, I needed some convincing. However, one bite was all it took. The unusual flavor as well as the low cost of ingredients makes this one a keeper.

Ingredient	Cost	Cost per recipe
4 tablespoons lemon juice	$0.10 per lemon	$0.10
2 tablespoons (1 oz) olive oil	$0.13 per ounce	$0.13
1 teaspoon (< .1 oz) cayenne pepper	$0.43 per ounce	$0.01
20 shrimp (14 oz)*	$0.39 per ounce	$5.46
Zest of one lemon	Included in lemon cost	$0.00
2 tablespoons (1 oz) butter	$0.12 per ounce	$0.12
1 cup (8 oz) cream	$0.09 per ounce	$0.72
Salt and pepper to taste	$0.00	$0.00
1 pound pasta	$0.03 per ounce	$0.48
½ cup (2 oz) Parmesan, grated	$0.66 per ounce	$1.32
Total Cost		**$8.34**

1. Preheat the grill.

2. Combine 2 tablespoons of the lemon juice, olive oil, cayenne pepper and shrimp. Toss to coat. Set aside.

3. Heat the remaining lemon juice, zest and butter over medium-high heat. Let bubble for 30 seconds.

4. Add the cream and salt and pepper to taste. Stir frequently until mixture has been reduced by half. Remove from heat.

5. Cook the pasta according to directions.

6. While pasta is cooking, grill shrimp for about 5 minutes.

7. Toss the pasta in the sauce over medium heat and add the grated cheese. Stir until cheese has melted.

Note: Without the shrimp this dish costs $0.72 per serving.

* Size of shrimp varies. For this recipe 5 shrimp = 2.5 oz.

Three Cheese Lasagna
6 servings @ $1.36 per serving

The combination of mozzarella and Swiss cheese in this recipe sets it apart from the usual ricotta varieties. If you don't like spicy, leave the red pepper flakes out.

Ingredient	Cost	Cost per recipe
1 pound hamburger	$0.15 per ounce	$2.40
1 onion, (8 oz) chopped	$0.01 per ounce	$0.08
4 garlic cloves, (.4 oz) chopped	$0.08 per ounce	$0.04
1 cup water	$0.00	$0.00
1 cup (8 oz) wine	$0.16 per ounce	$1.28
1 tablespoon (< .1 oz) oregano	$0.56 per ounce	$0.01
1 tablespoon (< .1 oz) basil	$0.50 per ounce	$0.01
1 tablespoon (< .1 oz) red pepper flakes	$0.22 per ounce	$0.01
12 ounces tomato paste	$0.06 per ounce	$0.72
8 ounces lasagna noodles	$0.05 per ounce	$0.40
1 ¼ cup (5 oz) mozzarella cheese, grated	$0.13 per ounce	$0.65
1 ¼ cup (5 oz) Swiss cheese, grated	$0.25 per ounce	$1.25
½ cup (2 oz) Parmesan cheese, grated	$0.66 per ounce	$1.32
Total Cost		**$8.17**

1. Fry hamburger in a large skillet. Add onion and garlic and fry until golden. Drain grease as necessary.

2. Add the water, wine, oregano, basil and red pepper flakes. Let it come to a boil and add the tomato paste. Reduce the heat, cover and simmer for about 1 hour.

3. Meanwhile, cook the noodles according to package directions. Drain and set aside.

4. Preheat oven at 350° F.

5. Spray a 9 x 13" pan with cooking spray. Put a little sauce on the bottom of the pan.

6. Put one layer of noodles on top of the sauce, followed by more sauce and the cheeses. Repeat with the second layer.

7. Bake for about 45 minutes. Let cool 10 minutes before slicing.

Note: This can be prepared ahead of time and frozen before baking. Allow it to thaw before baking. You may need to increase the cooking time if the noodles are still cold when you put it in the oven.

Steamed Fish with Orange Sauce and Asparagus
2 servings @ $2.64 per serving

I used to be a fish hater until my husband made this recipe. The fish is tender and the citrus sauce is a nice contrast. You can use halibut as well as mahi mahi.

Ingredient	Cost	Cost per recipe
3 oranges	$0.10 each	$0.30
1 tablespoon (1 oz) honey	$0.11 per ounce	$0.11
2 mahi mahi fillets (6 oz each)	$0.35 per ounce	$4.20
¼ onion (2 oz), sliced	$0.01 per ounce	$0.02
¼ teaspoon (< .1 oz) cayenne	$0.43 per ounce	$0.01
10 stalks of asparagus	$0.05 per ounce	$0.50
1 tablespoon (.5 oz) olive oil	$0.13 per ounce	$0.07
1 tablespoon (.4 oz) balsamic vinegar	$0.17 per ounce	$0.07
Total Cost		**$5.28**

1. Preheat oven to 425°.

2. Zest the oranges. Slice part of one orange to make 4 thin slices. Remove the rest of the segments. Juice the remaining 2 oranges. Put the zest, orange segments, juice and honey in a small pan and reduce on medium heat, about 10 minutes.

3. Lightly oil 2 pieces of parchment paper. Place a piece of fish on each. Top with sliced onion, cayenne and orange slices. Fold the ends of the paper in as if wrapping a sandwich.

4. Bake for 10 minutes. Pour orange sauce over the fish right before serving.

Asparagus:
1. Lay the asparagus in a single layer in a shallow pan.

2. Drizzle with olive oil.

3. Bake along side the fish for about 12 minutes, turning at least once.

4. Drizzle balsamic vinegar over the asparagus.

Sausage and Onion Calzones
4 servings @ $1.19 per serving

Don't be put off by making bread dough. This one is relatively easy, especially if you have a mixer with a dough hook. It is easy to adjust the dough by adding a little more water or flour as needed. A pizza stone is also a plus. I like to serve these with a bowl of spaghetti sauce on the side as a dip.

Ingredient	Cost	Cost per recipe
1 ½ cups warm water	$0.00	$0.00
1 tablespoon (.4 oz) dry yeast	$0.09 per ounce	$0.04
1 teaspoon (.2 oz) salt	$0.01 per ounce	$0.01
1 teaspoon (.2 oz) ounce sugar	$0.02 per ounce	$0.01
4 cups (1 lb) bread flour	$0.01 per ounce	$0.16
¼ cup (2 oz) olive oil	$0.13 per ounce	$0.26
10 ounces sausage	$0.09 per ounce	$0.90
1 onion (8 oz), chopped	$0.01 per ounce	$0.08
2 tablespoons (1 oz) butter for sauté	$0.12 per ounce	$0.12
2 cloves garlic, (.2 oz) chopped	$0.08 per ounce	$0.02
2 cups (5 oz) mushrooms, sliced	$0.12 per ounce	$0.60
½ cup (4 oz) fresh ricotta cheese	$0.12 per ounce	$0.48
1 ¼ cups (5 oz) mozzarella cheese, grated	$0.13 per ounce	$0.65
½ cup (2 oz) Parmesan, grated	$0.66 per ounce	$1.32
2 eggs	$0.06 each	$0.12
Salt & pepper to taste	$0.00	$0.00
Total Cost		**$4.77**

Dough:
1. Stir the yeast into warm water (105° to 115° F). Let rest about 5 minutes.

2. Add the salt, sugar, flour and olive oil.

3. Knead about 15 minutes until smooth. Add more water or flour as needed.

4. Put dough in a large bowl that has been coated with cooking spray. Cover with plastic wrap and let rise in a warm place until double, about 2 hours.

5. Preheat the oven to 400° F.

6. Divide the dough in half and roll each half into a circle on a lightly floured surface.

7. Spoon half of the filling slightly off center on each dough circle.

8. Brush a little beaten egg on the edges of the circle and fold the dough in half. Pinch the edges together.

9. Using a pastry brush, brush beaten egg over the top of each calzone and bake for 25-30 minutes until golden brown.

10. Immediately brush the calzone with olive oil and sprinkle garlic salt and Parmesan cheese on top. Let cool for about 5 minutes before cutting.

Filling:
Prepare filling while dough is rising.

1. Brown sausage in small skillet and set aside.

2. Caramelize the onion in a small amount of butter for about 10 minutes on medium heat. Add the chopped garlic and sauté with the onions for one minute.

3. Sauté the sliced mushrooms in small amount of butter for about 8 minutes.

4. Grate cheeses and combine with the ricotta in a large bowl.

5. Add one egg, sausage, onion mixture, mushrooms, salt and pepper to the cheeses and mix.

Grilled Polenta with Garlic Tomato Sauce
4 servings @ 21¢ per serving

I never liked mush, mainly because I never liked how the word sounded. Ordering mush in a restaurant would conjure up a picture of all kinds of unappetizing things all mashed up in a bucket. However, polenta sounds intriguing, Italian and trendy. It is also versatile, cheap and tasty. It can be made days ahead and sliced as needed, grilled, fried or baked with or without sauce. Don't be tempted to buy ready made polenta in the store. You will pay over $2.00 a pound compared to $0.39 a pound if you make it yourself.

Ingredient	Cost	Cost per recipe
4 ½ cups water	$0.00	$0.00
Pinch of salt	$0.00	$0.00
1 ½ cups (10 oz) coarse yellow cornmeal	$0.02 per ounce	$0.20
4 tablespoons (2 oz) olive oil	$0.13 per ounce	$0.26
14 ounces chopped canned tomatoes	$0.02 per ounce	$0.28
2 cloves (.2 oz) garlic	$0.08 per ounce	$0.02
2 tablespoons (1 oz) tomato paste	$0.05 per ounce	$0.05
1 tablespoon (.1 oz) red pepper flakes	$0.22 per ounce	$0.02
Salt and pepper to taste	$0.00	$0.00
Total Cost		**$0.83**

Polenta:
1. Bring the water to a boil in large saucepan. Add a pinch of salt.

2. Pour the cornmeal in a steady stream into the boiling water, stirring continuously. Reduce the heat to low and stir occasionally until cornmeal thickens, about 20 minutes, or until you burn yourself twice!

3. Spray a loaf pan with cooking spray and pour mixture into pan. Let set up for a few hours, or overnight, until cool.

4. Slice the polenta and brush with olive oil. Grill around 10 minutes per side.

Sauce:
1. Sauté garlic in a little olive oil.

2. Add tomatoes, tomato paste and red pepper flakes to the garlic. Salt and pepper to taste. Heat through and serve over polenta.

Note: Leftover sauce can be frozen. This sauce is great on pizza too.

Meatball Sandwiches
4 servings @ $1.54 per serving

Everyone likes a meatball sandwich, especially with loads of melted cheese on top. I make plenty of meatballs at one time and freeze them in small baggies for use as needed.

Ingredient	Cost	Cost per recipe
1 pound hamburger	$0.15 per ounce	$2.40
1 cup bread chunks (2 slices day old bread)	$0.08 per ounce	$0.08
2 garlic cloves (.2 oz), chopped	$0.08 per ounce	$0.02
¼ cup (1 oz) Parmesan Cheese, grated	$0.66 per ounce	$0.66
1 egg	$0.06	$0.06
1 tablespoon dried basil	$0.50 per ounce	$0.01
Salt and pepper to taste	$0.00	$0.00
¼ cup (2 oz) olive oil	$0.13 per ounce	$0.26
½ cup (4 oz) spaghetti sauce	$0.07 per ounce	$0.28
4 sandwich rolls (2.6 oz each)	$0.15 per ounce	$1.56
½ cup (2 oz) mozzarella cheese, grated	$0.13 per ounce	$0.26
½ cup (2 oz) Pecorino Romano cheese, grated	$0.29 per ounce	$0.58
Total Cost		**$6.17**

1. Soak the bread chunks in water. Wring out excess water.

2. Add bread chunks to hamburger, garlic, Parmesan cheese, egg, basil, salt and pepper in a large bowl. Mix well.

3. Heat oil in a large skillet over medium high.

4. Form meat into balls with your hands. When oil is hot, fry meatballs, turning occasionally until brown and cooked through. Drain on paper towels.

5. Heat oven on broil.

6. Heat spaghetti sauce on low in microwave.

7. Slice meatballs and arrange on sandwich rolls. Ladle sauce on top. Add cheese. Put under broiler until cheese is melted.

Pork Burritos
8 servings @ 77¢ per serving

Before you buy that next burrito for 5 bucks, consider making it yourself. Beef works just as well as pork in this recipe. The secret is to cook the meat until it is really tender and shreds easily. Freeze leftovers in small containers for quick meals. Naturally, guacamole and sour cream can do a lot to dress it up.

Ingredient	Cost	Cost per recipe
2 pounds pork loin or roast	$0.12 per ounce	$3.84
1 onion, (8 oz) chopped	$0.01 per ounce	$0.08
2 cups water	$0.00	$0.00
4 garlic cloves, (.4 oz) minced	$0.08 per ounce	$0.04
2 tablespoons (1 oz) olive oil	$0.13 per ounce	$0.13
½ cup (2 oz) ground chili powder	$0.22 per ounce	$0.44
½ teaspoon (.1 oz) salt	$0.01 per ounce	$0.01
½ teaspoon (< .1 oz) cumin	$0.20 per ounce	$0.01
8 flour tortillas (2 oz each)	$0.07 per ounce	$1.12
1 cup (4 oz) cheddar cheese, grated	$0.13 per ounce	$0.52
Total Cost		**$6.19**

1. Place pork, onion and water in a large pot. Bring to a boil. Reduce heat and cover. Simmer for about 1 1/2 hours or until meat pulls apart easily.

2. Remove pork from the broth and shred. Reserve broth. Add water to equal 2 cups if necessary.

3. Heat oil over medium heat. Add minced garlic and fry until golden. Add the pork.

4. Sprinkle flour over the pork. Add chili, salt, cumin and broth. Cook over medium heat until almost dry, about 30 minutes.

5. Spoon pork mixture onto warmed tortillas. Add grated cheese.

Puttanesca with Bacon, Tomatoes and Basil
4 servings @ 58¢ per serving

This recipe is not only delicious, it is a real meat stretcher and has just enough bacon flavor to be satisfying. I like to add quite a bit of cayenne or red pepper flakes to give it some zing.

Ingredient	Cost	Cost per recipe
2 tablespoons (2 oz) olive oil	$0.13 per ounce	$0.26
4 strips bacon, (4 oz) chopped	$0.13 per ounce	$0.52
14 ounces can diced tomatoes	$0.02 per ounce	$0.28
¼ teaspoon (< .1 oz) cayenne pepper	$0.43 per ounce	$0.01
Salt and pepper to taste	$0.00	$0.00
1 pound pasta, any shape	$0.03 per ounce	$0.48
¼ cup (10 leaves) fresh basil, chiffonade	$0.50 per ounce	$0.10
¼ cup (1 oz) Parmesan cheese, grated	$0.66 per ounce	$0.66
Total Cost		**$2.31**

1. Heat the olive oil over medium heat and fry the bacon until crisp.

2. Add the tomatoes, including the juice, a pinch of cayenne and salt and pepper to taste.

3. Sauté the tomato mixture on high until sauce thickens, about 10 minutes, stirring occasionally.

4. Cook pasta according to directions and drain.

5. Toss pasta in sauce.

6. Add fresh basil and Parmesan cheese just before serving.

Lemon Pepper Turkey Pitas
4 servings @ 66¢ per serving

Turkey pitas are my favorite way to use leftover turkey - especially around Thanksgiving time. If you make this ahead, add the lettuce and tomato right before serving.

Ingredient	Cost	Cost per recipe
4 cups (1 lb) cooked turkey, cubed	$0.06 per ounce	$0.96
½ cup (4 oz) mayonnaise	$0.06 per ounce	$0.24
½ cup (4 oz) sour cream	$0.09 per ounce	$0.36
½ onion (4 oz) chopped	$0.01 per ounce	$0.04
1 teaspoon (< .1 oz) lemon pepper	$0.09 per ounce	$0.01
Salt and pepper to taste	$0.00	$0.00
1 (3 oz) tomato, cubed	$0.06 per ounce	$0.18
½ cup (1 oz) lettuce, chopped	$0.03 per ounce	$0.03
½ cup Cheddar cheese, cubed	$0.13 per ounce	$0.26
4 pitas (1.7 oz each)	$0.08 per ounce	$0.54
Total Cost		**$2.62**

1. Mix turkey, mayonnaise, sour cream, onion, lemon pepper, salt and pepper.

2. Add the tomato, lettuce and cheese.

3. Cut pitas in half and spoon mixture into the pockets.

Soups

Bean Soup with Ham
4 servings @ 54¢ per serving

When I think of all the ham bones I threw away in the past, I could cry. This is the simplest soup to make and one of the best. I freeze it in cupfuls for lunch size portions.

Ingredient	Cost	Cost per recipe
1 pound great northern beans	$0.04 per ounce	$0.64
7 cups water	$0.00	$0.00
1 ham bone with meat (1.5 lbs)	$0.06 per ounce	$1.44
½ onion, (4 oz) minced	$0.01 per ounce	$0.04
½ teaspoon (< .1 oz) salt	$0.01 per ounce	$0.01
2 bay leaves (< .1 oz)	$0.55 per ounce	$0.01
Pepper to taste	$0.00	$0.00
Total Cost		**$2.14**

1. Rinse beans. Heat the beans and water to boiling in a large pot. Remove from heat and let stand for at least one hour.

2. Add the remaining ingredients and heat to boiling. Cover the pot. Reduce the heat and simmer for an hour or until the beans are tender. (Add more water if necessary, however too much will make a watery broth.)

3. Remove the bay leaves and the ham bone. Pick any meat off the bone and return it to the pot.

Grandma's Chicken Soup
4 servings @ 70¢ per serving

This is a simple soup recipe my grandma and my mother made. We call it "sick kid" soup because it seems to taste extra good when you are not feeling well. After boiling the chicken, I use some of the chicken meat in the soup and use the rest to make chicken salad, thus the chicken does double duty and the cost is cut in half. This soup freezes well so you can always have some on hand for the next sick kid or neighbor.

Ingredient	Cost	Cost per recipe
1 whole chicken (4 lbs)	$0.03 per ounce	$1.92
2 (8 oz each) onions	$0.01 per ounce	$0.16
1 teaspoon (.2 oz) salt	$0.01 per ounce	$0.01
2 celery stalks	$0.08 stalk	$0.16
3 teaspoons (.3 oz) chicken bouillon	$0.14 per ounce	$0.04
Pepper to taste	$0.00	$0.00
8 ounces tomato sauce	$0.02 per ounce	$0.16
8 ounces egg noodles	$0.04 per ounce	$0.32
Total Cost		**$2.77**

1. Put rinsed chicken in a large pan and cover with water.

2. Cut onions in half and add onions, salt, celery, bouillon and pepper to the pot with the chicken. Boil, skimming off any scum that forms.

3. Reduce heat, cover the pan and cook for about 1 1/2 hours. Chicken should be tender and fall off the bone.

4. Put a colander over a large bowl and drain. Discard the onion and celery.

5. Add tomato sauce and pepper to taste.

6. Cube some of the chicken, about 1 cup, and return it to the broth.

7. Cook the noodles according to the package directions and add to the broth.

8. Try not to slurp while you eat it.

Chunky Tomato Soup
4 servings @ 60¢ per serving

You'll never think about can soup the same way after tasting this recipe. The caramelized onions and garlic make it taste anything but tired.

Ingredient	Cost	Cost per recipe
4 strips (4 oz) bacon	$0.16 per ounce	$0.64
1 onion (8 ounces), chopped	$0.01 per ounce	$0.08
4 cloves (.4 oz) garlic, chopped	$0.08 per ounce	$0.04
14 ounces of can tomatoes	$0.02 per ounce	$0.28
1 can (10 ¾ ounces) tomato soup	$0.05 per ounce	$0.54
1 can (10 ½ ounces) chicken broth	$0.02 per ounce	$0.21
6 ounces tomato juice	$0.04 per ounce	$0.24
Pepper to taste	$0.00	$0.00
1 teaspoon (< .1 oz) dried basil	$0.50 per ounce	$0.01
¼ cup (2 oz) red wine	$0.16 per ounce	$0.32
1 tablespoon (< .1 oz) parsley, chopped	$0.06 per ounce	$0.01
Total Cost		**$2.37**

1. Cube the bacon and fry. Remove it from the pan and set aside.

2. Add onions and fry until golden brown.

3. Add garlic to onions and fry until garlic is light brown. Drain grease.

4. Combine the can tomatoes, tomato soup, chicken broth, tomato juice, pepper, basil and red wine in a large pot. Add the onion and garlic mixture. Heat through.

5. Ladle into bowls and sprinkle bacon and chopped parsley on top.

Potato Soup with Swiss Cheese and Ham
4 servings @ 53¢ per serving

This hearty soup is a meal in itself. Leftover soup can be frozen without a problem, assuming you have any leftover!

Ingredient	Cost	Cost per recipe
3 potatoes (1 lb), peeled and cubed	$0.01 per ounce	$0.16
1 onion (8 oz), chopped	$0.01 per ounce	$0.08
1 ½ cups water	$0.00	$0.00
3 cups (24 oz) milk	$0.02 per ounce	$0.48
1 teaspoon (.2 oz) salt	$0.01 per ounce	$0.01
3 tablespoons (1.5 oz) butter, melted	$0.12 per ounce	$0.18
2 tablespoons (.1 oz) parsley, minced	$0.49 per ounce	$0.01
2 tablespoons (.7 oz) flour	$0.01 per ounce	$0.01
½ cup (3 oz) cooked ham, chopped	$0.06 per ounce	$0.18
1 cup (4 oz) Swiss cheese, grated	$0.25 per ounce	$1.00
Pepper to taste	$0.00	$0.00
Total Cost		**$2.11**

1. Bring potatoes, onion, water and salt to a boil on high heat. Reduce heat, cover and simmer until potatoes are tender, about 20 minutes. Do not drain.

2. Mash potatoes with a fork. Add the milk.

3. In a bowl, blend butter, flour, parsley and pepper and add to potato mixture.

4. Cook and stir over medium heat until thickened.

5. Add ham and Swiss cheese. Stir until cheese is melted and serve.

Savory Mushroom Soup
4 servings @ 53¢ per serving

Every mushroom lover will love this soup. After tasting the fresh mushroom flavor, you will wonder why you ever bothered with the canned stuff!

Ingredient	Cost	Cost per recipe
2 cups (5 oz) mushrooms, sliced	$0.12 per ounce	$0.60
⅓ cup (2.3 oz) butter	$0.012 per ounce	$0.28
⅓ cup (1.3 oz) all purpose flour	$0.01 per ounce	$0.01
½ teaspoon (.1 oz) salt	$0.01 per ounce	$0.01
¼ teaspoon (< .1 oz) mustard powder	$0.46 per ounce	$0.01
2 cups (16 oz) chicken broth	$0.02 per ounce	$0.32
1 cup (8 oz) cream	$0.09 per ounce	$0.72
1 cup (8 oz) milk	$0.02 per ounce	$0.16
4 tablespoons (< .1 oz) chives, chopped	$0.14 per ounce	$0.01
Salt and pepper to taste	$0.00	$0.00
Total Cost		**$2.12**

1. Sauté the mushrooms in butter until tender, about 6 minutes.

2. Add the flour, salt and mustard powder and mix until blended.

3. Add the chicken broth and bring mixture to a boil. Cook and stir for one minute.

4. Reduce heat and add the cream and milk. Cook 3 to 5 minutes longer.

5. Ladle into bowls and add the chives. Add salt and pepper if desired.

Salads

BBQ Chicken Salad
4 servings @ 65¢ per serving

Chicken salad is always a staple at a picnic or at a bring-your-own dish buffet. The barbecue sauce in this dish makes the taste unusual. My friend likes to add hard boiled eggs, which I find despicable. Egg lovers will beg to differ I am sure. This recipe is a good use for left over chicken.

Ingredient	Cost	Cost per recipe
½ cup (4 oz) mayonnaise	$0.06 per ounce	$0.24
¼ cup (2 oz) barbecue sauce	$0.03 per ounce	$0.06
1 tablespoon (.3 oz) onion, minced	$0.01 per ounce	$0.01
Pepper to taste	$0.00	$0.00
1 tablespoon (.5 oz) lemon juice	$0.05 per ounce	$0.03
8 cups (16 oz) chopped lettuce	$0.50 per head (.3 per oz)	$0.48
2 (3 oz each) tomatoes, chopped	$0.06 per ounce	$0.18
½ cup (2 oz) Cheddar cheese, grated	$0.13 per ounce	$0.26
4 cups (1 pound) chicken, cooked	$0.03 per ounce	$0.48
6 slices (6 oz) bacon, cooked & chopped	$0.13 per ounce	$0.78
Total Cost		**$2.52**

1. Combine the mayonnaise, barbecue sauce, onion, pepper and lemon juice and chill until serving time.

2. Combine the lettuce, tomatoes, cheese and chicken

3. Just before serving, place salad on individual serving plates and spoon dressing over salad. Sprinkle with bacon.

Note: Left over turkey would work as well.

Fig Salad
2 servings @ 50¢ per serving

I never knew I liked figs until I tried them! This salad shouts gourmet in every bite. I always keep a supply of figs in the cupboard just for this dish. Although this recipe calls for lettuce, mixed greens is a nice change, though a little more expensive. You can substitute pecans or walnuts if you find a good price.

Ingredient	Cost	Cost per recipe
4 cups (4 oz) fresh spinach	$0.09 per ounce	$0.36
4 (1.3 oz) dried figs, sliced	$0.21 per ounce	$0.27
¼ cup (1 oz) red onion, chopped	$0.05 per ounce	$0.05
2 tablespoons (.5 oz) almonds, toasted & sliced	$0.20 per ounce	$0.10
2 tablespoons (.6 oz) feta cheese	$0.17 per ounce	$0.10
1 tablespoon (.4 oz) balsamic vinegar	$0.11 per ounce	$0.04
1 tablespoon (.7 oz) honey	$0.11 per ounce	$0.08
Total Cost		**$1.00**

1. Arrange the spinach on two plates and add the figs, onion, almonds and feta cheese.

2. Whisk together the balsamic vinegar and the honey and drizzle over the greens.

Greens with Cranberries and Walnuts
2 servings @ 44¢ per serving

This salad looks beautiful and the tastes of the various ingredients compliment each other well. I like to use mixed greens but any favorite greens will do.

Ingredient	Cost	Cost per recipe
5 cups (5 oz) mixed greens	$0.04 per ounce	$0.20
2 green onions, chopped	$0.08 each	$0.16
2 tablespoons (.6 oz) chopped walnuts, toasted	$0.18 per ounce	$0.11
2 tablespoons (.6 oz) feta	$0.17 per ounce	$0.10
2 tablespoons (.8 oz) dried cranberries	$0.25 per ounce	$0.20
1 tablespoon (.4 oz) raspberry chipotle sauce	$0.16 per ounce	$0.06
1 tablespoon (.7 oz) balsamic vinegar	$0.11 per ounce	$0.04
Total Cost		**$0.87**

1. Place the greens on two large salad plates.

2. Add the onion, walnuts, feta and cranberries.

3. Whisk the raspberry chipotle sauce and the balsamic vinegar together and drizzle on the salads.

Pomegranate and Pear Salad
2 servings @ 42¢ per serving

I love the taste as well as the color of pomegranates. When pomegranates are in season, buy plenty and freeze the seeds in small containers for later. Use the pomegranate molasses sparingly, as a little goes a long way. Try Asian pears for a different texture.

Ingredient	Cost	Cost per recipe
4 cups (2 oz) fresh spinach	$0.09 per ounce	$0.18
1 ripe pear (6 oz) sliced	$0.03 per ounce	$0.18
2 tablespoons (1 oz) pomegranate seeds	$0.07 per ounce	$0.07
2 tablespoons (.6 oz) feta cheese	$0.17 per ounce	$0.10
2 tablespoons (1.2 oz) pomegranate molasses	$0.26 per ounce	$0.31
Total Cost		**$0.84**

1. Arrange the spinach on two plates.

2. Add the sliced pear, pomegranate seeds and feta to the spinach.

3. Drizzle the pomegranate molasses over the salad.

Sweet Treats

Baked Pears
2 servings @ 44¢ per serving

You must give this recipe a try. It is a welcome change from the normal sweet and fattening desserts. I tried to cut down on the sugar but found that less sugar would not thicken the wine to my liking.

Ingredient	Cost	Cost per recipe
2 ripe pears (6 oz each)	$0.03 per ounce	$0.18
1/3 cup (3 oz) red wine	$0.16 per ounce	$0.48
1/3 cup (3 oz) sugar	$0.02 per ounce	$0.06
1/8 cup (.5 oz) Romano cheese, grated	$0.29 per ounce	$0.15
Total Cost		**$0.87**

1. Preheat oven to 400° F.

2. Slice a small amount off the bottom of the pear so that it can stand up. Place pears in a small oven proof pan.

3. Combine the wine and the sugar and pour over the pears.

4. Bake until pears are soft, about 20 minutes, depending on the ripeness of the pear.

5. Place pears on plates and allow them to cool.

6. Spoon the thickened wine mixture over the pears.

7. Grate Romano cheese over the pears.

Cinnamon Berry Crepes
7 servings (2 each) @ 65¢ per serving

Crepes are fun and easy to make and a great dessert to have ready in the freezer. I usually wrap them in stacks of 4 so I do not have to defrost all of them at once. Use whatever fruit is in season. Add a little whip cream and a drizzle of chocolate syrup on the plate for an elegant presentation.

Ingredient	Cost	Cost per recipe
1 cup (4 oz) all-purpose flour	$0.01 per ounce	$0.04
2 large eggs	$0.06 each	$0.12
1 cup (8 oz) milk	$0.02 per ounce	$0.16
⅓ cup (2.7 oz) butter, melted	$0.12 per ounce	$0.32
2 tablespoons (1 oz) granulated sugar	$0.02 per ounce	$0.02
Pinch of salt	$0.00	$0.00
½ cup water	$0.00	$0.00
2 tablespoons (1 oz) butter for brushing the pan	$0.12 per ounce	$0.12
1 ¾ (14 oz) heavy cream	$0.09 per ounce	$1.26
14 ounces of berries or your favorite fruit	$0.18 per ounce	$2.52
Cinnamon for dusting (< .1 oz)	$0.20 per ounce	$0.01
Powdered sugar for dusting (< .1 oz)	$0.02 per ounce	$0.01
Total Cost		**$4.58**

1. Put the flour, eggs, milk, butter, sugar, salt and water in a blender. Blend until batter is smooth, scraping the sides of the bowl as needed. (Add additional milk if the batter seems too thick.) Batter can be used right away or put in the refrigerator for later.

2. Melt the 2 tablespoons of butter. Warm a non-stick frying pan with a 7-inch bottom over moderate heat. When hot, brush with melted butter.

3. Using ¼ cup batter or less, tilt pan and pour batter onto one side, quickly rotating the pan so that the batter covers the entire bottom in a thin layer. When the crepe is lightly browned, flip it to the other side with fingers or spatula and cook for additional 30 to 45 seconds. Remove the cooked crepe, wipe out the pan and repeat.

4. When ready to serve, whip the cream, adding sugar if desired. Pipe the whip cream into the center of the crepe in a line. Place at least 4 berries on the cream. Gently roll the edges, making a long thin tube and place the crepe on the plate with edges down.

5. Sift a little cinnamon and powdered sugar on top and garnish with additional berries. Drizzle with chocolate syrup if desired.

Hazelnut Meringues
50 cookies @ 3¢ per serving

Store bought meringues give the real thing a bad name. I never realized how good they could be until I made them myself. Since meringues use only the egg whites, freeze the yolks for later and use them to make your dog some of his favorite biscuits. This recipe uses Frangelico, which is a wonderful hazelnut liqueur. If you prefer not to use it, you can find a hazelnut extract on the internet, but be sure to use a smaller amount. Meringues should be kept in air tight containers. Never freeze them as moisture will ruin them.

Ingredient	Cost	Cost per recipe
½ cup (2 oz) hazelnuts, toasted & chopped	$0.32 per ounce	$0.64
1 ½ cup (12 oz) granulated sugar	$0.02 per ounce	$0.24
6 egg whites, room temperature	$0.06 per ounce	$0.18 *
½ teaspoon (< .1 oz) cream of tartar	$0.94 per ounce	$0.01
3 tablespoons (1.5 oz) Frangelico	$0.30 per ounce	$0.45
Total Cost		**$1.52**

1. Preheat oven to 225°

2. Line a large baking sheet with parchment paper.

3. Chop the hazelnuts with a little sugar in a food processor.

4. Beat egg whites and cream of tartar in a medium bowl until soft peaks form.

5. Gradually add the remaining sugar, a little at a time, until stiff peaks form.

6. Add the Frangelico and stir gently.

7. Gently fold the nuts into the egg mixture.

8. Spoon the mixture into a piping bag fitted with a large star tip. Pipe the meringue onto the parchment paper.

9. Bake for 2 to $2\frac{1}{2}$ hours until dry. Cool completely and remove carefully.

Note: Because a liqueur is "heavier" than an extract, it may bead up near the bottom of the cookie, which does not affect the taste in the least.

* Remember: the cost is based on using only half of each egg.

Trail Mix Cookies
34 cookies @ 13¢ per serving

These cookies have become the favorite in my household, even surpassing chocolate chip cookies! The combination of all the ingredients gives them an interesting texture and flavor that comes through in every bite.

Ingredient	Cost	Cost per recipe
1 cup (8 oz) butter, softened	$0.12 per ounce	$0.96
1 cup (5.5 oz) light brown sugar	$0.03 per ounce	$0.17
⅔ cup (4.6 oz) granulated sugar	$0.02 per ounce	$0.09
¼ cup (3 oz) honey	$0.11 per ounce	$0.33
2 eggs	$0.06 per egg	$0.12
1 ½ teaspoon (.3 oz) vanilla	$0.14 per ounce	$0.04
2 ½ cup (10 oz) all purpose flour	$0.01 per ounce	$0.10
2 teaspoons (<.1 oz) baking soda	$0.03 per ounce	$0.01
1 teaspoon (<.1 oz) cinnamon	$0.20 per ounce	$0.01
1 teaspoon (<.1 oz) salt	< $0.01 per ounce	$0.01
½ cup (2.2 oz) sunflower seeds, toasted	$0.12 per ounce	$0.27
½ cup (1.8 oz) pumpkin seeds, toasted	$0.22 per ounce	$0.40
1 cup (4 oz) walnuts, toasted and chopped	$0.18 per ounce	$0.72
1 cup (3 oz) rolled oats	$0.05 per ounce	$0.15
½ cup (3.5 oz) m&ms	$0.13 per ounce	$0.46
¼ cup (.8 oz) cranberries, dried	$0.25 per ounce	$0.20
¼ cup (1 oz) raisins	$0.10 per ounce	$0.10
1 ½ cup (1.5 oz) rice crispy cereal	$0.09 per ounce	$0.14
Total Cost		**$4.28**

1. Preheat oven to 300° F.

2. Mix the butter, brown sugar, granulated sugar and honey until just combined. Add eggs and vanilla.

3. Combine flour, baking soda, cinnamon and salt and mix into batter.

4. Add seeds, nuts, oats, M&Ms, cranberries, raisins and rice crispy cereal until combined.

5. Use a 2 oz muffin scoop and scoop onto parchment lined cookie sheets.

6. Bake for about 20 minutes. Do not over bake.

Coffee Granita
2 servings @ 35¢ per serving

For some reason granita is an overlooked dessert. You can't beat it for cost and taste. It is great on a hot evening. Although most recipes call for espresso or strong black coffee, I have made it from regular strength coffee that is left over from breakfast. Consider it almost free in that case! If the coffee is not hot when you use it, be sure to warm it up before adding the sugar. Don't serve it until you are ready to eat it, as it melts quickly.

Ingredient	Cost	Cost per recipe
1 cup (8 oz) black coffee	$0.08 per ounce *	$0.02
¼ cup (2 oz) sugar	$0.02 per ounce	$0.04
1 tablespoon (.5 oz) Kahlúa	$0.56 per ounce	$0.28
½ cup (4 oz) cream	$0.09 per ounce	$0.36
Total Cost		**$0.70**

1. Mix sugar into hot coffee and stir until dissolved.

2. Add Kahlúa.

3. Pour mixture into a small shallow pan and place in the freezer.

4. Stir with a fork every 30 minutes for 3 hours, breaking up the ice into fluffy crystals.

5. Whip the cream, adding a little sugar if desired. Spoon granita into cups and add the whip cream.

* You will use approximately .2 ounces of ground coffee to make 1 cup of coffee. Price is based on ground coffee and not brewed coffee.

Steamed Fish

Jake's Dinner

Baked Pears

Turkey Pita

Greens with Cranberries and Walnuts

Pork Burritos

Mushroom Soup

Coffee Granita

Jake's Dessert

Cinnamon Berry Crepes

Breakfast Pizza

Polenta

Lemon Pasta

Trail Mix Cookies

Chicken Alfredo

Mushroom Frittata

Garlic Chicken Thighs

Ham and Spinach Pasta

BBQ Chicken Salad

Sausage Calzone

Jake's Favorite Dog Biscuits
25 three inch biscuits @ 3¢ per biscuit

If you don't like this recipe, there are thousands of dog biscuit recipes on the internet. It is also easy to invent your own. Either way, you will save money. Besides, they are fun to make and they smell great while baking. Try one. I did!

Ingredient	Cost	Cost per recipe
2 teaspoons (.2 oz) chicken bouillon	$0.14 per ounce	$0.03
¾ cup hot water	$0.00	$0.00
1 ½ cup (6.8 oz) whole wheat flour	$0.02 per ounce	$0.14
1 ¾ cup (8.8 oz) all purpose flour	$0.01 per ounce	$0.09
2 cloves garlic, (.2 oz) chopped	$0.08 per ounce	$0.02
1 egg	$0.06	$0.06
½ cup (4 oz) vegetable oil	$0.04 per ounce	$0.16
½ cup (1.5 oz) powdered milk	$0.15 per ounce	$0.23
1 tablespoon (.5 oz) brown sugar	$0.03 per ounce	$0.02
Total Cost		**$0.75**

1. Preheat oven to 350°.

2. Dissolve the chicken bouillon in hot water.

3. Mix together the wheat flour, all purpose flour, garlic, egg, oil, milk and brown sugar. Add the bouillon and water. Mix to form a soft dough.

4. Lightly flour work surface. Roll dough to desired thickness and cut with cookie cutter.

5. Bake on parchment paper for 40 minutes, or until dry and hard.

6. Store in air tight container.

Note: Don't be picky about the kind of oil you use, after all, it's for a dog's palate. I have used canola oil as well as French fry oil.

Price Calculation Rules

1. When possible, most items are given a price per ounce.

2. Spices such as salt and pepper, which are added as a pinch or used to season to taste are too small to measure and are given the price of $0.00.

3. Spice amounts which weigh less than .1 of an ounce or cost less than 1¢ per ounce are given the price of 1¢.

4. Items which are usually bought by the unit, such as lemons and eggs, are given the price of the unit.

5. Items which are usually bought by the bunch, such as green onions, are given the price per each or per bunch.

6. Fresh garlic is given the price of 1¢ per clove.

7. Water is given a price of $0.00.

8. Eggs that are separated and only the yolk or egg white are used are given ½ the price of the egg.

9. Weights of chicken pieces and fish can vary and are given an estimate. Chicken breasts are given the weight of 8 ounces. Chicken thighs are given the weight of 6 ounces. Fish is given the weight of 6 ounces.

10. For the most part, weights and dollar amounts are rounded up and down accordingly to the nearest tenth.

11. The following conversions apply for the recipes used:
1 cup of butter = 8 ounces or 2 sticks
1 cup of cheese = 4 ounces
1 cup of cream, milk, water = 8 ounces
1 cup of flour = 4 ounces
1 cup of fresh greens, spinach, lettuce = 1 ounce
1 cup of sliced mushrooms = 2 ounces
1 cup of sugar = 8 ounces
1 onion = 8 ounces
1 pear = 6 ounces
1 slice of bacon = 1 ounce
1 tablespoon of honey = .6 of an ounce
1 tablespoon of olive oil = 1 ounce
1 tablespoon of vinegar = .4 of an ounce

Ingredient Prices
(Prices reflect sales and coupon savings)

Item	Price per pound/per ounce/per bunch	Volume or unit equivalent
Almonds	$3.20/lb, $0.20/oz	¼ cup = 2 oz
Asparagus	$1.39/lb, $0.38/oz	1 stalk = $0.05
Bacon	$1.99/lb, $0.13/oz	1 slice = 1 oz
Baking Soda	$0.40/lb, $0.03/oz	1 tsp = < .1 oz
Balsamic vinegar	$0.11/oz	$1.79/16.9 fl oz, 1 Tbsp = 4 oz
Basil, dried	$0.50/oz	1 tsp = < .1 oz
Basil, fresh	$0.40/bunch, $0.50/oz	10 leaves = ¼ cup
Bay leaves	$0.55/oz	2 leaves = < .1 oz
BBQ sauce	$0.03/oz	$0.99/25.2 oz, 1.4 cup = 2 oz
Blackberries	$0.18/oz	$0.99/5.6 oz, 12 berries = 2 oz
Bread crumbs	$0.10/oz	$2.49/24 oz
Bread, white	$0.08/oz	$2.00/24 oz, 2 slices = 1 oz
Butter	$1.96/lb, $0.12/oz	2 Tbsp = 1 oz, 1 cup = 8 oz
Cayenne Pepper	$0.43/oz	
Celery	$0.77/bunch	10 stalks/bunch, $0.08/stalk
Cheddar Cheese	$2.11/lb, $0.13/oz	1 cup = 4 oz
Chicken Bouillon	$2.24/lb, $0.14/oz	1 tsp = .1 oz
Chicken breast, boneless	$1.99/lb, $0.12/oz	1 breast = 8 oz
Chicken broth	$0.32/lb, $0.02/oz	$0.21/14 oz
Chicken thighs	$0.77/lb, $0.05/oz	1 thigh = 6 oz
Chicken, whole	$0.55/lb, $0.03/oz	
Chile Powder	$0.22/oz	

Item	Price per pound/per ounce/per bunch	Volume or unit equivalent
Chives	$0.14/oz	$1.39/10 oz, Grow your own!
Cinnamon	$0.20/oz	
Coffee	$0.08/oz	$0.99/12 oz (great sale!)
Cornmeal	$0.39/lb, $0.02/oz	
Cranberries, dried	$3.99/lb, $0.25/oz	
Cream	$0.09/oz	$2.75 qt, 1 cup = 8 oz
Cream of Tartar	$0.94/oz	
Cumin	$0.20/oz	1 tsp = .1 oz
Egg Noodles	$0.04/oz	$0.25/7 oz
Eggs		$0.99/18 or $0.06 each
Feta	$2.99/lb, $0.17/oz	¼ cup = 1 oz
Fettuccine	$0.89/lb, $0.06/oz	
Figs, dried	$3.36/lb, $0.21/oz	$2.49/12 oz
Flour, all purpose	$0.17/lb, $0.01/oz	1 cup = 4 oz
Flour, bread	$0.18/lb, $0.01/oz	1 cup = 4 oz
Flour, wheat	$0.29/lb, $0.02/oz	1 cup = 4.5 oz
Frangelico	$0.30/oz	$20.00/750 ml
Garlic	$1.26/lb, $0.08/oz	1 clove = .1 oz
Great Northern Beans	$0.06/lb, $0.04/oz	$5.99/10 lbs
Ham	$0.99/lb, $0.06/oz	
Hamburger	$2.39/lb, $0.15/oz	
Hazelnuts	$5.19/lb, $0.32/oz	
Honey	$1.70/lb, $0.11/oz	¼ cup = 3 oz, 1 Tbsp = .7 oz
Kahlúa	$0.56/oz	$17.00/liter, 1 Tbsp = .5 oz

Item	Price per pound/per ounce/per bunch	Volume or unit equivalent
Lasagna noodles	$0.79/lb, $0.05/oz	
Lemon juice	$0.05/oz	
Lemon Pepper	$0.09/oz	$0.48/5.5 oz
Lemons	$0.010 each	
Lettuce	$0.36/lb, $0.03/oz	$0.50/head = 1.4 lbs, ½ cup = 1 oz
M&Ms	$2.08/lb, $0.13/oz	$6.99/52 oz
Mayonnaise	$0.96/lb, $0.06/oz	$2.00/32 oz
Mahi Mahi	$5.62/lb, $0.35/oz	
Milk	$2.36 gallon, $0.02/oz	1 cup = 8 oz, $0.15/cup
Mixed salad greens	$0.60/lb, $0.04/oz	
Mozzarella Cheese	$2.14/lb, $0.13/oz	1 cup = 4 oz
Mushrooms	$1.98/lb, $0.12/oz	1 cup = 2.5 oz
Mustard, yellow	$0.03/oz	1 cup = 2.5 oz
Mustard Powder	$0.46/oz	
Nutmeg, fresh	$1.37/oz	
Olive Oil	$0.13/oz	½ cup = 4 oz, 1 Tbsp = .5 oz
Onion, red	$0.79/lb, $0.05/oz	1 onion = 8 oz, ¼ cup = 1 oz
Onions, green	$0.50/bunch	6 in a bunch, $0.08 each
Onions, yellow	$0.01/oz	
Orange	$0.10 each	
Oregano, dried	$0.56/oz	
Parmesan Cheese	$10.55/lb, $0.66/oz	1 cup = 4 oz
Parsley, fresh	$0.49/bunch, $0.06/oz	1 bunch = 8 oz, 1 Tbsp = < .1 oz
Pasta	$0.50/lb, $0.03/oz	

Item	Price per pound/per ounce/per bunch	Volume or unit equivalent
Pears	$0.50/oz	1 pear = 6 oz
Pecans	$4.50/lb, $0.28/oz	
Pecorino Romano Cheese	$4.59/lb, $0.29/oz	1 cup = 4 oz
Pita	$0.08/oz	$0.79/10 oz, 6 in a bag
Pomegranate	$1.19/lb, $0.07/oz	1 pomegranate = 1 lb
Pomegranate Molasses	$0.26/oz	$2.59/10 fl oz
Pork Roast	$1.99/lb, $0.12/oz	
Potatoes	$0.10/lb, < .01/oz	$0.99/10 lbs
Powdered Milk	$0.15/oz	½ cup = 1.5 oz
Pumpkin Seeds	$3.59/lb, $0.22/oz	
Raisins	$1.59/lb, $0.10/oz	
Raspberry Chipotle Sauce	$0.16/oz	
Red Pepper Flakes	$0.22/oz	$0.48/2.2 oz, 1 Tbsp = .1 oz
Rice Crispy Cereal	$0.09/oz	$2.99/32 oz
Ricotta, fresh	$1.99/lb, $0.12/oz	½ cup = 4 oz
Rolled Oats	$0.05/oz	$2.29/42 oz
Salt	$0.12/lb, < $0.01 oz	1 tsp = .2 oz
Sandwich rolls	$0.11/oz	$2.25 per 8 rolls, 1 roll = 4.5 oz
Sausage	$1.50/lb, $0.09/oz	
Shrimp	$0.39/oz	5 shrimp = 3.5 oz
Sour Cream	$1.50/lb, $0.09/oz	½ cup = 4 oz
Spaghetti Sauce	$0.07/oz	
Spinach, fresh	$0.79/bunch, $0.09/oz	1 cup = 1 oz
Spinach, frozen	$1.19/lb, $0.07/oz	

Item	Price per pound/per ounce/per bunch	Volume or unit equivalent
Sugar, brown	$0.40/lb, $0.03/oz	1 cup = 1 Tbsp = .5 oz
Sugar, granulated	$0.32/lb, $0.02/oz	1 tsp = .2 oz, 1 cup = 8 oz
Sugar, powdered	$0.36/lb, $0.02/oz	1 lb = 4 cups
Sunflower Seeds	$1.99/lb, $0.12/oz	
Swiss Cheese	$3.99/lb, $0.25/oz	1 cup = 4 oz
Tomato Juice	$0.04/oz	
Tomato Paste	$0.06/oz	$0.33/6 oz
Tomato Sauce	$0.02/oz	
Tomato Soup	$0.05/oz	$0.50/10 3/4 oz
Tomato, fresh	$0.89/lb, $0.06/oz	1 tomato = 3 oz
Tomatoes, can	$0.02/oz	
Tortillas	$0.07/oz	$1.29 /10 (17.5 oz package)
Turkey	$0.99/lb, $0.06/oz	
Vanilla	$0.14/oz	$36.59/32 fl oz
Vegetable oil	$0.04 oz	1 cup = 8 oz
Walnuts	$1.50/lb, $0.09/oz	
Wine, red	$0.16/oz	$3.99/750 ml, 1/3 cup = 3 oz
Yeast	$1.50/lb, $0.09 0z	1 Tbsp = .4 oz, 2 1/4 tsp = .5 oz

BONE APPÉTIT!

CPSIA information can be obtained
at www.ICGtesting.com
Printed in the USA
LVHW071440300420
654804LV00022B/680